COMPOSER
SHOWCASE
HAL LEONARD
STUDENT PIANO LIBRARY

Celebration Suite

ORIGINAL DUETS FOR ONE PIANO, FOUR HANDS

BY EUGÉNIE ROCHEROLLE

CONTENTS

ISBN 978-1-4950-5080-0

HAL•LEONARD®
CORPORATION

7777 W. BLUEMOUND RD. P.O. BOX 13819 MILWAUKEE, WI 53213

In Australia Contact:
Hal Leonard Australia Pty. Ltd.
4 Lentara Court
Cheltenham, Victoria, 3192 Australia
Email: ausadmin@halleonard.com.au

Visit Hal Leonard Online at
www.halleonard.com

Across the Years

By Eugénie Rocherolle

4

In Defense of Liberty

By Eugénie Rocherolle

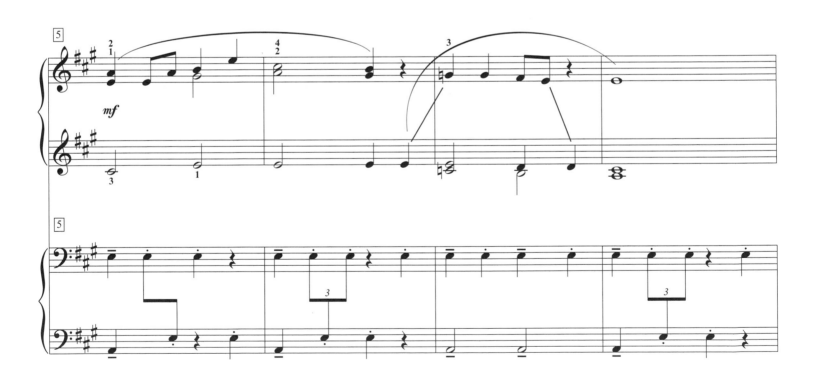

Andante (♩ = 96)

mp con dolore

15

Journey in Space

By Eugénie Rocherolle

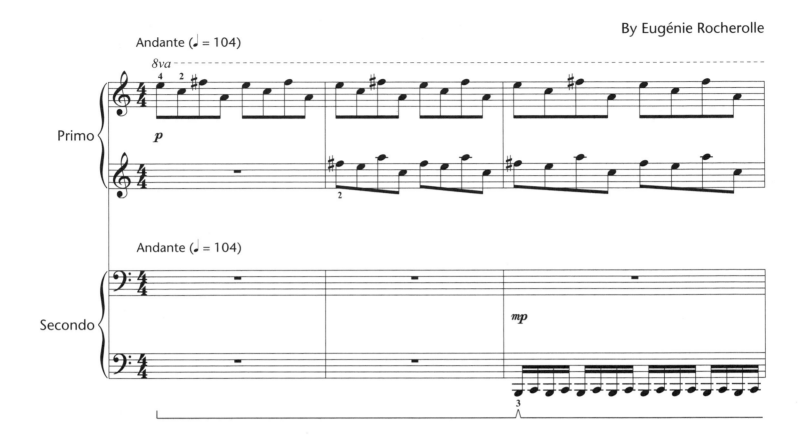